This journal is given to

____

on __________________________

from _________________________

Grandma's Story

Your date and place of birth:

Your parents' names:

Your brothers and sisters, from oldest to youngest:

Names of other close family members:

Date and place you married Grandpa:

Grandpa's parents' names:

His brothers and sisters, from oldest to youngest:

My parents' birth dates and places of birth:

My aunts and uncles, from oldest to youngest:

Our Family History

Where is your side of the family originally from?

How did they get to this country?

What were their occupations once they arrived?

Where is Grandpa's side of the family originally from?

Tell me about some of our more interesting family members.

What are some of the biggest challenges or setbacks our family has faced?

How did we get through them?

What is something I may not know about our family?

Which physical family traits do I have?

What personality traits have I inherited?

Who do I most remind you of in our family?

What were you like as a child?

What were you most interested in as a little girl?

Who did you resemble from your family?

Where did you live when you were a child?

What did your parents do for a living?

Did you have a nickname growing up?

Who gave it to you, and why?

Who were your best friends when you were little?
What were they like?

Did you have any pets growing up? Tell me about them.

What types of games did you like to play?

What were your favorite toys? Why did you love them so?

What were your favorite books?

What were your favorite songs?

Tell me about a time you got into real trouble when you were younger.

What did you fight about with your brothers and sisters?

What are some modern inventions that you would never have dreamed of back then?

Growing Up

What did your family do in the evenings for entertainment?

What was a hard lesson you had to learn?

Tell me about a special memory you have of your mother.

Tell me about a favorite memory of your father.

What is one of the best memories you have of your grandmother?

What is one of your favorite memories of your grandfather?

What did you want to be when you grew up?

Who were your heroes, and why?

What were your favorite subjects in school?

What did you dislike about school?

What were your after-school activities?

As a teenager, what kind of music did you listen to?

What were some of your favorite movies?

What did you worry about most as a teenager?

Describe a fun evening spent with your friends.

Who was your very first date? Where did he take you?

Starting a Family

How did you meet Grandpa?

What were your first impressions of him?

If someone had told you early on that you were going to marry Grandpa, what would you have said?

Where did you and grandpa go on your first date? What do you remember most about it?

How did Grandpa ask you to marry him?

Tell me about the wedding ceremony and who was in the wedding party.

After the ceremony, how did you celebrate?

Did you go on a honeymoon? If so, where?

Where did you live as newlyweds?

Did you work? If so, what did your job entail?

How did you celebrate your first anniversary?

What is the most important thing you have learned about marriage and relationships?

Which aspects of marriage have surprised you the most?

Name all of the places you've lived in your lifetime.

A New Baby

How did Grandpa react when you told him he was going to be a father?

What was the best part about being pregnant with Mom/Dad?

How did you choose a name for Mom/Dad?

What other names did you consider?

How did having a child change your life?

Did you have any jobs while you were raising your children? If so, what were they?

Did you have any time to yourself during those years?

What activities or hobbies did you pursue?

Who did Mom/Dad look like when she/he was a baby?

What were Mom's/Dad's first words?

Tell me about some other firsts.

What were Mom's/Dad's favorite childhood toys?

What were some favorite stories and songs?

What is your favorite embarrassing story about Mom/Dad?

What were some hard lessons you learned as a parent?

What career path did you think Mom/Dad would pursue when she/he grew up?

As a child, how did Mom/Dad most often get into trouble?

What was Mom/Dad like when she/he was a teenager?

Tell me about a time when Mom/Dad made you proud.

What did you think when my parents first announced they were getting married?

What was the most memorable part of their wedding ceremony?

What was your reaction when you heard I was on the way?

What sort of parental advice did you give to my mom and dad?

When was the first time you saw me? How did you feel?

Who do you think I most resembled as a baby?

What kinds of games did we play together when I was little?

What did I show an early preference for?

What career paths did you see in my future?

Did I ever embarrass you in public? If so, tell me about it.

What is an unexpected perk of being a grandma?

What is your favorite family holiday, and why?

Tell me about a favorite holiday tradition in our family.

Which holiday traditions would you like to see me continue?

What is one of your favorite gifts from me?

Tell me about a time when you have been particularly proud of me.

What do you say when people ask about me?

What is one of your favorite ways to spend time with me?

What do you think is the most important lesson you have taught me?

Do you see similarities between us when you were my age?

In what ways are we different?

How am I like my parents?

Tell me about a time when I really wore you out.

If there were only one thing you could teach me, what would it be?

What is something that I have taught you?

What is one thing that you always want me to remember about you?

Notes